FIGHTING TO SURVIVE NATURAL DISASTERS
TERRIFYING TRUE STORIES

By Michael Burgan

COMPASS POINT BOOKS
a capstone imprint

Fighting to Survive is published by
Compass Point Books, an imprint of Capstone.
1710 Roe Crest Drive, North Mankato, Minnesota 56003
www.capstonepub.com

**Library of Congress Cataloging-in-Publication Data is available
on the Library of Congress website**
ISBN: 978-0-7565-6429-2 (hardcover)
ISBN: 978-0-7565-6568-8 (paperback)
ISBN: 978-0-7565-6430-8 (ebook pdf)

Summary: Describes the terrifying true stories of people who survived terrible
natural disasters such as tornadoes, earthquakes, hurricanes, and other storms.

Editorial Credits
Aaron J. Sautter, editor; Terri Poburka, designer; Morgan Walters, media researcher;
Kathy McColley, production specialist

Photo Credits
Alamy: Ajax News & Feature Service, 37, Sergey Yakovlev, 57; Associated Press:
Ramon Espinosa, File, 29; Getty Images: Haydn West - PA Images, 38, Keystone, 40,
TIM SLOAN, 14, Topical Press Agency, 45; Newscom: abaphotos770322, 51, Alvin
Baez/REUTERS, 22, JERRY MENNENGA/Rapport Press, 9, 12, Keystone Pictures
USA/ZUMA Press, 27, Koichi Kamoshida/ZUMAPRESS, 48, Kyodo, 47, MIKE
RANSDELL/MCT, 13, OLIVIER PAPEGNIES/Photoshot, 30, TIM HYNDS/Rapport
Press, 11, Xavier Araujo GDA Photo Service, 21; Shutterstock: Alexandr Zyryanov,
55, AridOcean, 6, arindambanerjee, 26, Daniel Prudek, 59, Frans Delian, 5, irabel8, 35,
Isaac Marzioli, design element throughout, JEAN-FRANCOIS Manuel, 19, lavizzara,
17, Miloje, design element throughout, pavalena, 42, 52, Peter Hermes Furian, 24,
Rafal Cichawa, 25, Rainer Lesniewski, 16, Ronnie Chua, Cover, Todd Shoemake, 7,
WillWight, 15, xpixel, design element throughout, yspbqh14, 43

All internet sites appearing in back matter were available and accurate when this
book was sent to press.

Printed and bound in the USA.
PA99

TABLE OF
CONTENTS

INTRODUCTION

Hurricanes can hit land with the destructive energy of hundreds of powerful bombs. Violent earthquakes can shake entire cities and destroy buildings in seconds. The largest quakes can also launch giant waves called tsunamis. These deadly walls of water can destroy entire coastlines and kill thousands of people.

Around the world, disasters like these can happen at any time. For example, an average of 1,368 earthquakes are detected somewhere on Earth every day. Thankfully, most earthquakes are small. Only about 100 each year cause serious damage. Hurricanes, blizzards, and other powerful storms are less common. But the worst can cause billions of dollars in damage—and take many lives.

With some natural disasters, people have time to seek safety before their lives are in danger. But at times, the disasters strike with little or no warning. People might find themselves struggling to stay alive long enough to be rescued. Learn the incredible stories of brave people who found ways to survive in the middle of deadly natural disasters.

In 2004 a huge earthquake created a giant tsunami that caused widespread destruction in several countries around the Indian Ocean. More than 225,000 people were killed in the disaster.

A TERRIBLE TWISTER
THE BOY SCOUTS AT LITTLE SIOUX SCOUT RANCH

June 11, 2008, was a rainy day at the Little Sioux Scout Ranch in Monona County, Iowa. About 95 Boy Scouts, along with Scout leaders and local staff, were at the ranch that day. Some of the best Scouts from western Iowa, eastern Nebraska, and southern South Dakota had gathered there for leadership training. Just the day before, Scout leader Fred Ullrich had taught the boys how to give first aid. However, the Scouts didn't realize how soon they'd be putting their emergency medical training into action.

As dinner time approached, the skies began growing darker. Around 6:15 p.m., camp ranger Nathan Dean heard reports that a powerful thunderstorm was nearby. Iowans such as Dean

knew that the worst storms could produce deadly tornados. Less than two months before, a twister packing winds of more than 200 miles (322 kilometers) per hour had ripped through Butler County. It had killed nine people. When he heard that a rotating cloud was spotted near the ranch, Dean sounded the siren to alert the Scouts to take shelter. Dean couldn't know where the tornado might hit, but he wanted to warn everyone just in case.

DID YOU KNOW?

Tornadoes are often the most destructive storms on Earth. They can have wind speeds up to 300 miles (483 km) per hour. The biggest tornadoes can cut a path 1-mile (1.6-km) wide or more and travel along the ground for up to 50 miles (80 km). Tornadoes most often form in strong thunderstorms called supercells. During the storm, warm air rises into the clouds. At the same time, cooler air sinks toward the ground. The movement of the rising and falling air spins faster and faster until it creates a tornado. In the United States, tornadoes are most common in flat regions between the Rocky and Appalachian Mountains. Part of this area is sometimes called Tornado Alley because so many tornadoes

TERROR AT THE CABIN

Most of the campers and staff headed to
two separate cabins to take shelter. In the north
cabin, about 50 Scouts ate a spaghetti dinner and
then made plans to watch a movie. As the Scouts
debated which movie to watch, Fred Ullrich burst
through the cabin door. "Get under the tables!" he
shouted. The Scouts scrambled to obey his order.
When a tornado hits, people often seek safety
in basements or shelters designed to handle the
twister's fierce power. But at the ranch, the tables
in the cabin offered the only protection.

As the wind picked up, Ullrich went outside
to shut the cabin door. Then he saw part of the
cabin's roof blow away. He thought to himself,
"I hope that's all that happens." But then he felt the
wind pick him up and toss him to the side.

Inside the cabin, the Scouts tried to hold onto the tables,
but the tornado blew away the tables as the walls began to
crack. On one side of the cabin, a stone chimney crumbled to
the ground, pinning some Scouts in the rubble.

Ethan Sande was one of the boys crushed beneath the
stone. He blacked out for a few moments. When he woke up,
he felt rain on his face. He struggled to breathe as some of the
other Scouts worked to free him. Lying across him was another

The tornado completely destroyed the north cabin while the Scouts tried to take shelter inside.

Scout. Sande wasn't sure who. But he could see the boy wasn't moving, and Sande soon realized that he was dead.

Outside the cabin, Scout leader Ullrich got up off the ground. As quickly as the powerful winds had hit the ranch, they quieted again. Ullrich couldn't hear in one ear, and he realized that a stone had lodged in it. He pulled it out and surveyed the scene. Some boys, like Sande, were trapped under the collapsed chimney. Others were under the walls. Several cried in pain.

TRYING TO HELP

Ullrich quickly put his training into action. He began to organize the uninjured Scouts to help the others. Some Scouts used their own T-shirts to wrap the wounds of the injured boys. Others tried to help boys who had gone into shock. Seeing one Scout pinned under bricks and wood, Ullrich used a long iron bar to pry off the rubble.

Back inside, some of the older scouts quickly sprang into action. T. J. Claussen tried to treat the wounded. But he could tell he was injured himself—his ribs ached, and he had trouble breathing. Nearby, Jacob Vogts helped some of the wounded boys, while Alex Robertson covered them with blankets. Robertson could tell that some Scouts were seriously hurt, with broken bones or worse. Ullrich saw that some of the boys had been killed. He covered their bodies and kept the other Scouts focused on helping each other. He tried to reassure the Scouts, saying, "Help is on the way."

At the south cabin, the tornado's winds had ripped up trees, but the building itself survived. Matt Bentz and the others inside could hear the Scouts at the north shelter calling for help. However, their leaders told them to stay inside until they knew it was safe to leave. Meanwhile, Nathan Dean's cottage on the ranch had been destroyed, though he and his family were safe. They had taken shelter in a closet and had somehow survived when the house collapsed around them. Three Scouts helped rescue them from the rubble and then took an all-terrain vehicle to the other cabin to help there.

The twister destroyed several cabins and trees at the ranch.

TREATING THE WOUNDED

The first rescue workers arrived a short time after the tornado hit. They cut through downed trees blocking the road. Emergency medical and rescue teams came from three states to help at Little Sioux. Altogether, the storm had injured 48 people at the ranch. Helicopters flew out five of the wounded, while others were driven to local hospitals.

Ethan Sande was one of the more seriously wounded Scouts. The hospital where the rescuers took him was jammed with injured boys. Sande soon learned that he had several broken bones in his hip and spine, as well as some broken ribs. Even some of his teeth were knocked out. For some time after the storm, he had to use a wheelchair. As he said years later, "I had to learn to walk again."

Emergency workers arrived soon after the tornado struck to help the injured victims.

Scout leaders studied the damage done by the tornado's fierce winds.

    T. J. Claussen learned that he also had broken ribs and back bones, along with a collapsed lung. But he and Sande survived. Four of the Scouts who had been with them in the north shelter were not so lucky. The falling stones and cement blocks killed Aaron Eilerts, Josh Fennen, Sam Thomsen, and Ben Petrzilka. All were 13 or 14 years old.

A TORNADO'S POWER

Soon after the storm tore through the ranch, weather officials knew just how powerful the tornado had been. Its winds were at least 145 miles (233 km) per hour, and it had cut a path a quarter-mile (0.4 km) wide and 14 miles (23 km) long. The twister had flipped a tractor trailer and ripped out trees, but the only deaths were the four boys killed at the ranch.

After the June 2008 tornado, the Boy Scouts rebuilt the Little Sioux Ranch. They also added two tornado shelters designed to withstand the most powerful tornadoes. Donations of more than $1 million helped pay for the new shelters.

President George W. Bush met the Scouts and Scout leaders at the White House on July 31, 2008. He honored them for their bravery after surviving the deadly tornado.

DID YOU KNOW?

The Little Sioux tornado was listed as an EF3 on the Enhanced Fujita scale. The scale shows how powerful a tornado's winds are. It's named for T. Theodore Fujita, who created an early version of the scale in 1971. The EF Scale rates a tornado's strength by the amount of damage it caused. The EF Scale has six categories, based on a tornado's wind speed:

Rating	Wind Speed
EF0	65 to 85 mph (105 to 137 kph)
EF1	86 to 110 mph (138 to 177 kph)
EF2	111 to 135 mph (178 to 217 kph)
EF3	136 to 165 mph (218 to 266 kph)
EF4	166 to 200 mph (267 to 322 kph)
EF5	201 mph and up (323 kph and up)

THE MENACE OF MARIA
CARMEN CHÉVERE ORTIZ

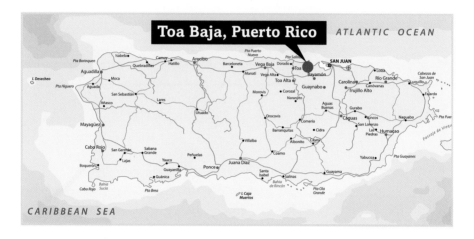

Some disasters strike in an instant without any warning. But as Hurricane Maria churned through the Caribbean Sea in September 2017, the residents of Puerto Rico knew a deadly storm was on the way. They'd heard about the damage the storm caused to the U.S. Virgin Islands and Dominica nearby. Maria had hit there as a Category 5 hurricane—the strongest possible. The storm's top winds in Dominica had reached 160 miles (257 km) per hour. After tearing through the smaller islands, Maria was headed directly for Puerto Rico.

Carmen Chévere Ortiz—Milly to her friends—knew all about the power of hurricanes. She had lived for decades in Toa Baja, just west of Puerto Rico's capital of San Juan. When Ortiz was a young girl in 1979, Hurricane David had hit the island and flooded her neighborhood. Her father had picked her up and carried her through the streets. The water was so high it still lapped against her feet.

Since then Ortiz had lived through several other big hurricanes. Hurricane Hugo struck Puerto Rico in 1989, killing 12 people and causing $1 billion worth of damage. In 1998 Hurricane Georges was only a Category 1 storm when it hit Puerto Rico. But the storm moved slowly across the island. It dropped nearly 30 inches (76 centimeters) of rain and caused severe flooding.

Hurricane Maria

DID YOU KNOW?

Like tornadoes, hurricanes are rated on a scale. It's called the Saffir-Simpson Hurricane Wind Scale. It rates hurricanes from 1 to 5 based on the storms' sustained wind speeds.

Storm Category	Wind Speed
Category 1	74 to 95 mph (119 to 153 kph)
Category 2	96 to 110 mph (154 to 177 kph)
Category 3	111 to 129 mph (178 to 208 kph)
Category 4	130 to 156 mph (209 to 251 kph)
Category 5	157 mph (252 kph) and up

ADVANCED WARNINGS

Just two weeks before Hurricane Maria, another major storm had brushed Puerto Rico's northern coast. Like Maria, Hurricane Irma had first caused severe damage in the Virgin Islands. Puerto Rico escaped a direct hit, but parts of the island felt Irma's 100-mile- (161-km-) per-hour winds. Four people died during the storm. Still, Ortiz had survived all those hurricanes. The Puerto Rican government opened hundreds of storm shelters to keep people safe. But Ortiz and many other Puerto Ricans chose to stay in their homes as Maria approached. They ignored Governor Ricardo Rosselló's warning on September 19: "It is time to act and look for a safe place if you live in flood-prone areas or in wooden or vulnerable structures."

DID YOU KNOW?

When a major hurricane approaches land, government officials often tell people to evacuate. Their property can't be saved from a direct blow, but their lives can be saved. Unfortunately, some people choose to stay in their homes. In 2005 when Hurricane Katrina hit New Orleans, Louisiana, it caused massive destruction. The city's mayor had ordered everyone to leave. But tens of thousands of people stayed. Many didn't have cars. Others had no money to stay in hotels. Some sick, disabled, and elderly people could not be moved easily. Their family members chose to stay and take care of them. For these and other reasons, many residents were still in New Orleans when Katrina hit. The huge storm caused terrible flooding. More than 1,800 people along the Gulf Coast died. Most of them were in and around New Orleans.

MARIA PACKS A PUNCH

On the morning of September 20, Hurricane Maria hit the southern coastal town of Yabucoa. With winds of 155 miles (249 km) per hour, it was now a Category 4 storm, but just barely. It worked its way northwest across the island, heading toward Toa Baja. As the storm raged, Ortiz saw water from a nearby creek start to cover her neighbor's patio. As the water rose rapidly, she remembered the flooded streets of her neighborhood during Hurricane David nearly 40 years before. "This is a place that floods," she thought to herself. Ortiz gathered her mother and six children. Together they headed to the family's vehicle. The flooding water nearly covered the car's rear wheels, and the water stank from sewage. As she drove through the rising waters, Ortiz called out the window, "The river is coming! Get out! Get out!"

Before hitting Puerto Rico, Hurricane Maria's fierce winds destroyed thousands of buildings on Dominica and the U.S. Virgin Islands.

Along the streets of Toa Baja, people moved to the second stories of their homes, hoping to escape the flood. The winds had ripped off the roofs of some houses. As Ortiz drove, she saw ocean water coming ashore. It added to the flooding from a canal that flowed through the town. The rising waters now surrounded many homes. Ortiz decided she had to seek the highest spot in Toa Baja—the local school.

SAFETY IN A SCHOOL

By now some of Ortiz's neighbors were following her family, and they joined her at the school. The school was behind a locked gate. Some of the flood refugees said they shouldn't try to break in. But Ortiz was determined to find safe shelter for everyone trying to escape the still-rising waters. She found a heavy metal hook on a tow truck near the fence and used it to smash the locks until the gate opened.

As the day went on, more residents learned about the shelter now open at the school. They made their way through the flooded streets. Some people brought their pets, including a pig. The school soon had a new name—el Arca, or the Ark. It referred to the Bible story of the ark that Noah built to save people and animals from a worldwide flood.

As she had done outside the school, Ortiz took command inside the Ark. "Nobody is going to come for us," she told some neighbors. Then she broke into the kitchen to get food for everyone. As night came, she assigned people to sleep in different classrooms and recorded their names. Some people used window curtains as blankets to keep warm. Others huddled around a fire Ortiz's son lit in a cooking pot, using cardboard for fuel.

The floodwaters from the hurricane reached up to 20 feet (6 m) high. City streets, cars, and people's homes were covered in a thick coat of mud.

Through the night, more people kept arriving at the Ark. Some had been rescued from their flooded homes by a local fisherman nicknamed Teté. He used his small boat to ferry people to safety. By morning, Ortiz had a list of 200 names of people staying at the school. She and the others were still not sure when—or if—help would come. As Ortiz said later, "We were prepared to die."

MARIA'S DESTRUCTIVE POWER

Five days after the storm hit, Toa Baja's mayor, Bernardo Márquez García, came to the Ark. He convinced most of the people to move to an official shelter, with Ortiz still in charge. The people who went to the new shelter stayed there for about three weeks.

During that time, Ortiz realized how destructive Maria had been. The floodwaters had been as deep as 20 feet (6 m) in spots. Ortiz and her neighbors lost everything in their homes. The biggest problem across Puerto Rico was the loss of power and the lack of clean water. The entire island had lost electricity. Two months later, half the island still lacked power. And across the island, downed trees, debris, and landslides blocked almost all of the roads.

Ortiz's neighborhood finally got electricity back in March 2018, about six months after the storm. Volunteers began cleaning and repairing damaged homes. Ortiz's was one of the first repaired,

Hurricane Maria destroyed most of Puerto Rico's power lines. It took months for electricity to be restored across the island.

and she continued to help her neighbors who still struggled after the storm. She took donated food and supplies and gave them to anyone in need. After a U.S. magazine reported on Ortiz's efforts, she received praise for her heroism. Chelsea Clinton, the daughter of former president Bill Clinton, called her "an American hero."

Sadly, almost 3,000 Puerto Ricans didn't survive Maria. In the first days after the storm, Puerto Rican officials said only a few dozen people had died. But surviving a hurricane means more than escaping flood waters and high winds. In the months after the storm, many people died in the poor conditions. A lack of electricity and fresh water puts sick and elderly people at greater risk. Unfortunately, this is just what happened in Puerto Rico. Since the island nation is a territory of the United States, the U.S. government provided money and training to help Puerto Ricans be better prepared if another superstorm hits.

DID YOU KNOW?

In 1953 the U.S. National Hurricane Center started naming hurricanes in the Atlantic Ocean. Using a name was easier than trying to give a hurricane's specific location, especially if several storms were in the same area. If a hurricane is especially deadly or destructive, its name is not used again. The names Katrina, Irma, and Maria, for example, will never be given to another storm.

BURIED ALIVE

EVANS MONSIGNAC

Port-au-Prince, Haiti.

The work day was almost over for Evans Monsignac on January 12, 2010. He had spent the day selling rice at an outdoor market in Port-au-Prince, Haiti's capital city. The country is located on the Caribbean island of Hispaniola, which it shares with the Dominican Republic. Monsignac was sweating under the canvas awning that protected him from the sun. Even in January, temperatures in Port-au-Prince can easily reach close to 90 degrees Fahrenheit (32 degrees Celsius).

Like many Haitians, Monsignac worked many hours each day to support his family. Many poor people lived very close to one another in Port-au-Prince. They struggled to live on just $1 or $2 a day. Monsignac had risen at 5:00 a.m. that morning so he could reach the market and sell his rice.

There are several popular street markets in Port-au-Prince, Haiti, where people can buy food, clothing, artwork, and gifts.

Just before 5:00 p.m., he was finishing up with his last customer when he felt the first tremors. Then the ground began to shake, and a building behind him started to collapse. Concrete blocks began to fall around Monsignac. A powerful earthquake was shaking the whole city. He knew he should run, but before he could take action, the ground opened up under him. He prayed to God, "I have two children, please save me!"

As Monsignac lay in the hole, the falling concrete blocks pinned his legs. He could move his arms just a little and turn his head from side to side. But he was trapped in the rubble. It was dark all around, and he could hear the screams of other people stuck under the falling buildings. After a time the screaming stopped, and Monsignac guessed he was the only one still alive.

SEARCHING FOR SURVIVORS

Similar scenes were repeated across Port-au-Prince. An earthquake with a magnitude of 7.0 had struck just outside the city. It took only 20 seconds to flatten buildings everywhere. Soon cries for help and gray dust from crumbling concrete filled the air. Since demolished buildings had toppled into the streets, efforts to rescue those trapped in the rubble were slowed.

Over the next several days, about 1,500 rescue workers from several countries searched for anyone who might have survived. Some people caught in the rubble managed to send text messages to let their families know they were alive. One 7-year-old girl was trapped in a grocery store. Luckily, there was enough food in the store for her to eat until help came five days later on January 17.

BURIED IN THE RUBBLE

Back at the market, Evans Monsignac wasn't so lucky. Although he was still alive, he had no food. But he did have water. Some wells in the market had broken during the quake. Water seeped out of them toward Monsignac. He knew the water wasn't clean. The wells held water that had been used to wash clothes. But he also knew he needed to drink to stay alive. He cupped his hands, caught some of the dirty water, and brought it to his lips. It tasted horrible, but he drank it anyway. Later, he felt sick, but still he tried to drink small amounts of water.

The powerful earthquake reduced thousands of buildings to rubble.

As the days passed, Monsignac could smell the decaying bodies of dead people buried near him in the rubble. He tried to lay straight and not move. He didn't want the concrete blocks to shift and crush him. As he grew weaker, he sometimes passed out. When he was awake, he had no sense of time, and he was convinced he would die. Sometimes, he wished he would die. He couldn't see how he would survive much longer in the rubble. Other times, he made up little songs that he sang out loud, asking for God to roll the rocks off his trapped body.

DID YOU KNOW?

Scientists classify the strength of earthquakes by their magnitude. With a magnitude of 7.0, the 2010 Haiti quake was considered a major earthquake. On the scale, each level of earthquake is considered 10

The huge earthquake that hit Chile in 1960 cause massive destruction.

times more powerful than the level below it. So a magnitude 8.0 quake would be 10 times stronger than the one that hit Haiti. The most powerful earthquake ever recorded had a magnitude of 9.5. It struck southern Chile in 1960 and killed more than 1,600 people. The quake created a tsunami that reached as far away as the Philippines.

LUCKY TO BE ALIVE

In the city, the search effort for survivors went on. One mother who survived the quake went back to her flattened apartment building. She was determined to find her son, who had been missing since the quake hit. Amazingly, on January 22, she heard her son call out to her from the rubble. She sent rescue workers to pull him out. He had been buried in the building for 10 days. That same day rescue workers found an 84-year-old woman.

After that point, the rescue teams thought it would be unlikely to find any more survivors. On January 23, the Haitian government said official rescue efforts were over. The rescue workers had found 132 people. Elizabeth Byrs of the United Nations said the teams still there would act, if "there is the slightest sign of life." But she added, "Except for miracles, hope is unfortunately fading."

DID YOU KNOW?

Earth's crust is broken into slabs of rock called plates. The plates sit on Earth's mantle, which is a thick layer of rock and magma. Heat deep within Earth causes the top part of the mantle to move slightly. That movement makes the plates of Earth's crust move too. Earthquakes occur where two plates collide or slide against each other. The places where two faults slide against each other is called a strike-slip fault. Haiti sits near one of these faults. In the United States, a famous fault is the San Andreas Fault, which sits under western California.

But a miracle seemed to happen a few days later. On January 27 people in the Carrefour Feuilles neighborhood heard a female voice calling weakly from under some debris. Soon, local residents were chipping away at the rubble with shovels, hammers, and any other tools they could find. Haitian Red Cross volunteers and a French rescue team arrived to continue the digging. Finally, 16-year-old Darlene Etienne was pulled from the wreckage. Covered in white dust, she was dehydrated and needed oxygen. Unlike Evans Monsignac, she had never passed out while buried under the rubble. She had screamed for help, but no one had heard her. She said after she was found, "I could hear people passing by and I thought they were going to rescue me. But it was never me that they were rescuing."

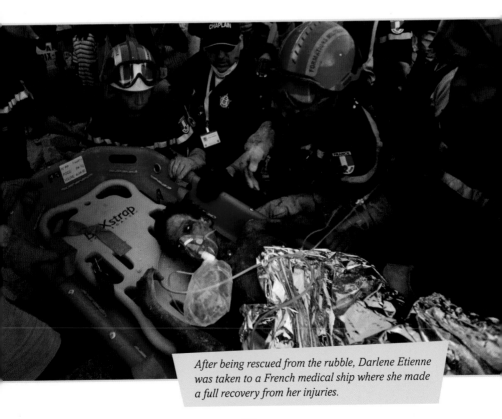

After being rescued from the rubble, Darlene Etienne was taken to a French medical ship where she made a full recovery from her injuries.

AN AMAZING STORY OF SURVIVAL

The people of Port-au-Prince continued searching and clearing the city's rubble. They hoped to recover the bodies of the dead. On February 8, people going through the debris by Evans Monsignac's old market made a startling discovery—the rice seller was still alive! He had wasted away while he was buried under the concrete. He was very thin, and his feet were covered with open wounds. He was also speaking nonsense as the rescuers pulled him out. But the little bit of dirty water he drank had been enough to keep him alive.

Rescue teams worked tirelessly for weeks to find any survivors trapped in the rubble.

Monsignac was taken to a hospital in Tampa, Florida. It took weeks for him to recover from the lack of food and water. At times he asked the doctors treating him to let him die because he was suffering so much. Other times, he showed signs of confusion. He thought his family had sold him into slavery. By the end of May, he was still in some pain, but he was eating solid food and beginning to walk again.

Monsignac's story amazed doctors. He is thought to have survived longer than anyone who has ever been buried alive in an earthquake. He was truly one of the lucky ones after the 2010 quake. As many as 300,000 Haitians died from the disaster. The devastation also left more than 1 million people homeless. As the country began to rebuild, it tried to make sure new buildings would be strong enough to withstand future quakes.

DID YOU KNOW?

Earthquakes slightly more powerful than the 2010 quake hit Haiti in 1751 and 1770. In 2018 a smaller earthquake centered off the northwest coast killed at least 15 people. Haiti has also been in the path of several killer hurricanes. Hurricane Jeanne caused floods that killed 3,000 people. Hurricane Flora hit in 1963, killing more than 8,000 Haitians. More recently, Hurricane Matthew killed more than 500 people and caused almost $3 billion in damage in 2016.

SURVIVING A STORMY SEA
NICK WARD

Sailing had been part of Nick Ward's life since he was a child in Hamble, England. As Ward grew up, he dreamed of sailing in the Fastnet Challenge Cup. This famous race started in 1925 and is held every two years. It takes sailors on a 608-nautical mile (1,126-km) course through the English Channel and across the Irish Sea, to a spot along Ireland's coast called Fastnet Rock. There the ships turn around and make their way back to England.

In August 1979, 23-year-old Ward finally got the chance to sail in the famous race. However, he didn't know that a terrible disaster awaited him and the rest of the crew on the *Grimalkin*. At just 30 feet (9 m), the *Grimalkin* was one of the smallest boats in the race. David Sheahan, the boat's owner and captain, led the six-man crew. Along with Ward were Sheahan's son Matt, Dave Wheeler, Mike Doyle, and Gerry Winks.

When the crew set sail on Saturday, August 11, they had calm waters and a sunny sky. Ward loved the boat and got along well with the rest of the crew. If he had any worries, it might have been about his health. Years before, he had developed epilepsy after experiencing severe bleeding in his brain. The disorder can cause people to have seizures and unusual behavior. But Ward made sure to bring enough medication to get him through the voyage.

On Sunday, the winds were lighter than the crew would have liked, but they were predicted to pick up during the day. On Monday, the winds increased and the *Grimalkin* reached a speed of about 10 knots, or almost 12 miles (19 km) per hour. Later that afternoon, several hours before sunset, the crew admired an orange-and-red glow in the sky. Matt Sheahan said, "I wonder what it means . . . more wind or less?" No one replied, because no one knew the answer.

DID YOU KNOW?

The force of winds at sea are ranked from 0 to 12 on the Beaufort Scale. It's named for Francis Beaufort, a British admiral during the 1800s. Beaufort based the scale on how much winds of different speeds filled the sails of his ship. Weather experts later attached a range of wind speeds to each force level, along with a description of the sea's surface. For example, a Force 10 storm creates high seas with large waves. Wind speeds are measured in knots. One knot equals 1.15 miles (1.85 km) per hour. The U.S. Weather Service added five extra force levels in 1955 for the five classes of hurricanes.

Force	Type of Wind	Wind Speed (knots)
0	calm	<1
1	light air	1–3
2	light breeze	4–6
3	gentle breeze	7–10
4	moderate breeze	11–16
5	fresh breeze	17–21
6	strong breeze	22–27
7	near gale	28–33
8	gale	34–40
9	strong gale	41–47
10	storm	48–55
11	violent storm	56–63
12–17	hurricane	64 and above

A STORM APPROACHES

The weather forecast that came late Monday afternoon gave a clue about the upcoming weather. The British Broadcasting Company (BBC) predicted that winds could increase to 46 miles (74 km) per hour. That would be a strong wind, but nothing the boat and crew couldn't handle. But a later forecast from a French source said the winds could reach up to 63 miles (102 km) per hour. The crew became worried. Winds that fast meant rough seas—perhaps too rough for the *Grimalkin*. But then another radio report came in saying the BBC forecast was correct. Captain Sheahan decided that the boat would sail on.

However, the sailors on the *Grimalkin* and other yachts didn't know that a small storm in the North Atlantic sea was about to turn into a huge and destructive one. And it was heading right for the boats sailing for Fastnet Rock.

By about 9 p.m. Monday night, Nick Ward felt the waves growing larger. He accidentally knocked into the captain as he walked across the cabin below deck. "It's building faster than we expected," Sheahan said. As Ward prepared to go on deck, the captain instructed him to clip on his safety harness. It would keep him attached to the boat if a wave tossed him overboard. On deck, Ward saw water spilling into the cockpit. But he, like the others, counted on the BBC forecast. They thought the *Grimalkin* should have no problem getting through the night.

POWERFUL WIND AND WAVES

However, the crew soon realized that the BBC forecast was wrong. They watched as the anemometer, which measures wind speed, went up to near Force 10. The sailors inflated their life jackets and began taking down the mainsail. Reducing the amount of sail exposed to the wind is a standard safety measure during a storm. Then the crew closed up the cabin so water wouldn't flood the sleeping area and the boat's supplies. They couldn't turn back, as the *Grimalkin* was too far from shore and the seas were too rough. The crew had to ride out the storm as the winds whipped harder and the waves increased. Ward glanced at the anemometer and saw that the wind was now at close to 75 miles (120 km) per hour—hurricane strength.

The wind pushed the boat through the water so fast that it began to vibrate. Early on Tuesday morning, a wave towering 10 feet (3 m) above the crew's heads smashed into the *Grimalkin*. It flattened the boat against the water. It was the first of several knockdowns, meaning the ship's mast was parallel with the ocean surface. The boat eventually righted itself. But more knockdowns followed through the night. One almost flipped the boat so that the cockpit was underwater. Thanks to their harnesses, the sailors stayed attached to the boat through it all.

In high winds and rough seas, boat crews take down the sails for safety. Then they take shelter inside the sealed cabin to wait out the storm.

A FIGHT TO LIVE

Around 5:30 a.m. Tuesday morning, the first signs of daylight appeared. But the storm continued to rage. The sailors were shivering after being drenched in cold ocean water, and Ward saw that the others' faces were pale. The waves were now as high as 50 feet (15 m), and the crew had no control over the *Grimalkin*'s course. Another knockdown came, stronger than the others. It tossed Ward into the sea, and a sharp pain shot through his leg. He looked back and saw David and Matt Sheahan on the boat, calling to him, "Come on Nick, pull yourself up. You can do it." But Ward's hands were now raw and bloody. He let go of the safety line, and the *Grimalkin* dragged him through the water. With the others' help, Ward managed to get back on board. As he coughed up water, he realized he could have easily drowned.

David and Matthew Sheahan went down into the cabin to send out a Mayday call for help. While they were below, another giant wave rocked the boat, sending the Sheahans bouncing around the cabin. Matt came out on the ladder from the cabin, shouting, "Dad is injured." The rest of the crew could see blood spouting from a wound on the captain's head. Ward also noticed water beginning to fill the cabin.

The crew got David Sheahan into the cockpit and tried to treat his wound. The blow to his head had knocked him senseless, although he was still conscious. Matt insisted that they use the boat's life raft to try to get his father help. Nick Ward resisted—he had been taught to never leave a boat unless it was sinking. For a time, the men argued about what to do. But in the end, all the crewmembers except Gerry Winks agreed with Matt. Winks had been injured in an earlier knockdown and was unable to talk.

The crew began to prepare the lifeboat when another giant wave smashed into the *Grimalkin*. The boat rolled completely over, snapping the mast. When the boat came right-side up, Ward was thrown into the water again. He called for help, but no one responded. With a push from another wave, he managed to crawl back onto the boat. But the life raft was gone, and so was the rest of the crew. Looking over the side of the *Grimalkin*, Ward saw Winks in the water, unconscious. He pulled Winks into the boat and began breathing

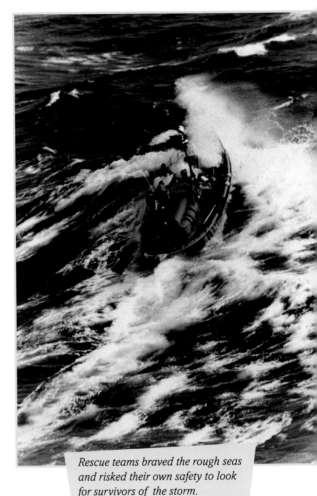

Rescue teams braved the rough seas and risked their own safety to look for survivors of the storm.

into his mouth, hoping to keep him alive. Winks began breathing again, but barely. He struggled to speak and finally told Ward, "If you ever see [my wife] again tell her I love her." And then he died. Ward was alone on the *Grimalkin*. His leg was injured, his head was battered from the knockdowns, and the storm still raged all around him.

ALONE ON THE WATER

For a moment, Ward cried for his dead friend. But he had little
time to think about Winks. Soon, the biggest wave yet picked
up the boat's stern, or rear, and flipped it end over end. It was like
the boat was doing cartwheels, which sailors call pitch-poling. Still
attached to his harness, Ward flew through the air, then landed
hard on Winks's dead body. A bit later, Ward heard the sound
of engines above him. Somewhere in the clouds, an airplane
was looking for boats in trouble. Ward wanted to get the plane's
attention, but the crew
had already used up all
the boat's emergency
flares. And he didn't
have a working radio
to send out a Mayday
signal. Fighting his
injuries and the cold,
Ward began to talk
to his dead friend.
He took out all his anger
and frustration in a
one-way conversation
that dragged on and on.

*A memorial in Ireland honors the
memory of the sailors who died in
the 1979 Fastnet Race disaster.*

Ward later realized that he hadn't eaten or drunk anything in hours. He went into the cabin and searched for something to eat. He found a can of pineapples, but he had no way to open it. He finally saw a sealed carton of milk floating in the water-filled cabin. The water was contaminated, but Ward plucked the carton out of the water and drank the milk. Nothing had ever tasted better to him.

To try to get water out of the cabin, Ward grabbed a bucket. He filled it again and again and dumped it over the side of the boat. Bailing out the water helped him focus on something other than the storm and the possibility of death. But as the storm continued to batter the *Grimalkin*, the water kept slowly rising.

DID YOU KNOW?

Boats float because of a force called buoyancy. When an object is less dense than water, the water pressure pushes it up, causing it to float. But too much weight can cause a boat to sink. That's why Nick Ward tried to bail out the water

RESCUED AT LAST

By Tuesday afternoon, Ward saw some blue patches in the sky—the storm was passing. But the seas were still rough. His spirits rose when he heard another plane overhead. Unfortunately, it couldn't spot the boat through the remaining clouds. As evening approached, Ward spotted a large ship in the distance. He blew his safety whistle and jumped up and down. He waved his arms, hoping someone on the ship would spot him. But the vessel was too far away, and the *Grimalkin* was too small for anyone to see it on the still-thrashing waves.

Nick Ward was rescued after surviving alone for more than 12 hours aboard the Grimalkin *in the middle of stormy seas.*

The sun set, with Ward still unsure if he would ever be spotted and rescued. Then he heard a sound overhead. It was the whirr of a helicopter's blades. Soon a British Navy sailor descended on a wire lowered from the chopper to the boat. Nick Ward was saved.

When he reached dry land, Ward learned that Matt Sheahan, Mike Doyle, and Dave Wheeler had been rescued in the lifeboat. David Sheahan had died after a wave had carried him away from the *Grimalkin*. Ward also discovered that he was the last of the 136 Fastnet sailors to be rescued. Almost 40 years after surviving the terrible storm, Ward told a newspaper that the events he experienced have "been in my head for many many years…. I wake up with it every morning."

DID YOU KNOW?

After the 1979 Fastnet disaster, race organizers made several changes to protect future sailors from huge storms. Boat captains must prove their experience and take a sea survival course. The race organizers also required new boat designs that would be less likely to capsize. Some of the greatest safety improvements came with new technology. Weather satellites above Earth allow for better forecasts, and captains have faster access to changing weather information. Boats also carry GPS devices, which can relay

A WALL OF WATER
DAVID CHUMREONLERT

David Chumreonlert
knew it would be a big
day for his students
at Nobiru Elementary
School. He had come to
Japan from Texas
in 2009 to teach
English, and he worked
at four schools in
Higashi-Matsushima.
The town sits close to
Matsushima Bay.

March 11, 2011,
was the last day of the
school year. The next day, Chumreonlert's students at Nobiru would
attend a graduation ceremony in the school's gym. He was excited
for the students, and he brought his camera to school to photograph
them as they rehearsed for the ceremony.

The day was almost over when Chumreonlert felt the school
shake. Soon he heard the principal shout, "This is a big one, so
everyone get under a desk." Chumreonlert knew earthquakes were
always a threat in Japan. Just eight years before, Higashi-Matsushima
had experienced three quakes on the same day. Japan has a long
history of devastating earthquakes. The worst occurred in 1923, in
the Japanese capital of Tokyo. It killed more than 100,000 people.

With sandy beaches and pine-covered islands, Matsushima Bay is considered one of Japan's most beautiful locations.

The quake that Chumreonlert and his students felt passed quickly, and it didn't seem to do much damage. Still, the class followed the principal's instructions and headed to the gym. About 200 people gathered there, including some parents who had come to Nobiru to pick up their children. Some elderly residents from a nearby nursing home also sought safety in the gym. Suddenly, a man burst into the gym yelling, "Tsunami is coming!"

THE POWER OF A TSUNAMI

Chumreonlert wondered how much danger a tsunami posed. The huge and destructive waves of water are often created by earthquakes. But the school was about 2 miles (3.2 km) from the coast, and the gym had been specially built to withstand tsunamis. Still, children and adults began climbing onto a stage at the back of the gym. Meanwhile, others climbed stairs that led to a balcony.

Then, looking through the gym's glass doors, Chumreonlert saw the tsunami coming. He watched as the massive wave rolled over the cars in the parking lot and headed right for the gym. The wave carried one car into the doors, smashing the glass. Chumreonlert joined the others and headed for the stage as the water poured into the gym, creating a whirlpool. From the stage, Chumreonlert watched the water rise. He saw chairs and desks floating in the water and heard the screams of panicked children as the water approached the stage.

DID YOU KNOW?

Powerful tsunamis have crashed into Japan for at least 1,300 years. More tsunamis have struck Japan than any other country. Tsunami is a Japanese word that means "harbor wave." One of the worst tsunamis struck Japan in 1896. It killed 22,000 people. More recently, in 2004, a magnitude 9.1 quake unleashed history's deadliest tsunami in the Indian Ocean. It struck Indonesia, Thailand, and other countries in the region. It killed at least 225,000 people

The people of Higashi-Matsushima and other towns along Japan's coasts know how dangerous tsunamis can be. After a huge earthquake in 1923, a 40-foot (12-m) wave had carried several thousand people out to sea. The Japanese know that when earthquakes strike, tsunamis are likely to follow. People should run for high ground as quickly as possible. But trapped in the gym, Chumreonlert and the others couldn't escape this tsunami.

In 1923 a powerful 7.9 magnitude earthquake destroyed much of Tokyo, Japan. More than 140,000 people died in the disaster.

TRYING TO HELP OTHERS

Chumreonlert could feel the sucking power of the whirlpool now spinning in the center of the gym. He held onto the stage wall tightly and watched the water carry two people toward him, a woman holding onto an elderly man. The man grabbed Chumreonlert's shoulder and clung tightly. But then the couple lost their grip, and Chumreonlert lost sight of them in the churning water. He grabbed onto the stage curtain, and then saw a set of wooden stairs float by. Chumreonlert jumped onto the stairs as if they were a life raft. But they offered no protection from the whirlpool of water still spinning inside the gym.

Chumreonlert realized that the balcony offered the best protection from the rising waters. He jumped off the floating stairs and managed to swim toward the balcony's railing. He was surprised to find something sturdy under his feet. It might have been the rim of the gym's basketball hoop. Chumreonlert stood on whatever it was and grabbed the balcony railing with one hand. He looked around the gym and saw that most of the children had safely reached the balcony. Others were still swimming toward it.

Then he spotted one of his students struggling to reach the balcony. As the student neared his teacher, Chumreonlert reached out and grabbed him, pulling him toward the balcony railing. Others on the balcony helped Chumreonlert get the boy over the railing. Then he spotted a woman floating by, tightly holding her baby. Chumreonlert managed to get them to safety too.

Chumreonlert then heard someone calling his name. He looked over and saw four of his students and a woman hanging onto a desk floating in the water. "Help us! Help us!" the children cried. The desk was out of reach, but it slowly drifted toward Chumreonlert. One by one, he grabbed each of the students and helped get them onto the balcony, followed by the woman.

Water from the tsunami created a deadly whirlpool of swirling debris inside the Nobiru Elementary School gymnasium.

THE EFFECTS OF THE TSUNAMI

Chumreonlert finally pulled himself onto the balcony, where he saw that some people still needed help. A teacher and some other adults were trying to get to the balcony from the stairs. Chumreonlert tried to help them and found himself back in the water. He realized now how cold it was, and he shivered as he helped people onto the balcony.

The powerful tsunami smashed cars and pushed mud and debris against the city's elementary schools.

Finally, the water from the tsunami stopped pouring into the gym. The water slowly began to drain from the building. But as night came, Chumreonlert and the others were still trapped inside. As they waited for rescuers, they sat in darkness. The gym had lost power when the earthquake struck. And the shaking wasn't done yet. Smaller quakes called aftershocks rocked the gym through

the night. With each shock, the survivors huddled together, seeking to calm their fears. Chumreonlert tried to comfort his students. "Hang in there, hang in there," he said with a smile.

It took almost two days for Chumreonlert to get out of the gym and back home. Outside the school, he could see how destructive the tsunami had been. A canal nearby was filled with cars and wrecked homes. The huge wave had been deadly for many people trapped inside the gym too. Not all had reached the safety of the balcony. About 85 died.

EARTHQUAKE AFTERMATH

The earthquake that struck off the coast of Japan on March 11, 2011, had a magnitude of 9.1. It was the strongest quake to ever hit the country. Scientists estimated that Japan's main island, Honshu, was pushed eastward about 8 feet (2.4 m). The waves of the tsunami that followed reached up to 30 feet (9 m) high. About 18,000 people were reported dead or missing after the one-two punch of the quake and tsunami. More than 120,000 buildings were destroyed and many more were damaged. Six years after the quake, 50,000 people were still living in temporary shelters.

After the tsunami, David Chumreonlert married a Japanese woman and moved to Sendai, not far from Higashi-Matsushima. He eventually quit teaching and began working as a land surveyor. For a time after the tsunami, Chumreonlert continued to help others affected by the disaster. He served as a translator for Americans who came to help the tsunami survivors.

Damage at the Fukushima Daiichi Nuclear Power Plant after the 2011 earthquake and tsunami

DID YOU KNOW?

South of Higashi-Matsushima, in Okuma, the tsunami severely damaged the Fukushima Daiichi Nuclear Power Plant. The damage caused the release of harmful amounts of radiation. The dangerous radiation forced about 100,000 people to leave their homes. The Japanese government has removed and secured millions of cubic feet of topsoil near Fukushima because of the radiation. They also cut down more than 200 acres (81 hectares) of trees. Water filled with radiation also entered the Pacific Ocean. Some fish ate radioactive food, but scientists found that the levels of radiation in these fish weren't dangerously high.

LOST IN A BLIZZARD
SURVIVING THE TIEN SHAN MOUNTAINS

For William "Spook" Spann, the hunting trip of a lifetime was coming to an end. Spann had traveled with his father, Dennie Spann, and their friend Clay Lancaster to the Central Asian country of Kyrgyzstan. The three men were deep in the country's remote Tien Shan mountains. They had gone out hunting on horseback for almost two weeks. Local guides helped them navigate the deep snow, which grew deeper every day. Now, on March 13, 2004, the hunters and their support team were beginning a 36-hour trip. They were headed to the nearest town about 300 miles (483 km) away.

The Spanns, from Tennessee, had planned this trip for months and had spent almost $15,000 each for it. Lancaster, from Canada, was a hunter and recorded the trip on his video camera. Leaving the base camp, they rode in a mini-van. But the vehicle got stuck after just a few hundred feet. The wind was whipping the snow into drifts up to 7 feet (2.1 m) deep. The Kyrgyz guides told the three hunters to instead join them in the remaining vehicle—an old, heavy, six-wheeled army truck.

SLOW PROGRESS

For a time, the truck was able to chug through the snow. But after just 1 mile (1.6 km), even this heavy vehicle bogged down and had to stop. The men got out, shoveled the snow, and pushed the truck free. But as the blizzard raged, the truck got stuck again and again. Spook Spann recalled, "It just snowed and snowed and snowed and snowed."

As the day went on, the storm worsened. The truck could barely move without getting stuck. The hunters and their team had gone too far to turn back. They decided to stop for the night. All the men huddled in the back of the truck, which was covered only with a canvas tarp. That night, the temperature fell to -40° F (-40° C). Inside the truck, the hunters worried about the extreme cold and running out of food. They wondered if they'd ever get out of the mountains.

DID YOU KNOW?

Extreme cold can be dangerous for people who aren't prepared for it. The first concern is frostbite. It affects skin exposed to cold and windy weather. The cold shuts down the flow of blood to parts of the body, such as the fingers and toes. In extreme cases, the cells in the body's tissues will freeze, leading to cell death. Affected body parts may have to be surgically removed. Hypothermia is another serious problem. In cold conditions a person's body temperature will start to fall. At first it causes pain in parts of the body. Then the person will begin to feel numb and lose feeling in the hands and feet. If the body isn't warmed up in time,

A FIRST RESCUE

In the morning, the men woke up to see their truck was
completely snowed in. Lancaster went outside and saw whiteout
conditions—it was impossible to tell the ground from the sky. He
had a satellite phone with him, but the battery was almost drained.
Lancaster managed to call his brother and tell him their GPS
coordinates. But then the battery died.

As the day passed, the men ate the last of their food and burned
whatever they didn't need for heat. That night, they drew close
together again in the truck to share their body heat and keep warm.
The temperatures once again plunged to -30° F (-34°
C) or colder. The men wondered what would happen
to them. Dennie Spann later recalled, "It was definitely
a concern of mine that if somebody does get to us, are
they gonna get to us in time?"

The next morning Lancaster debated whether to
leave the truck and look for help or stay and hope for
rescue. With the weather clearing, he decided to stay,
and the decision proved to be a good one. Soon the men
heard the thumping rotors of a large helicopter. It was
an old Russian chopper designed to carry supplies and
troops. The helicopter landed near the stranded truck.
Three Kyrgyz officials stepped out of the aircraft and
gave the hunters and their team food and water. When
they finished eating, the men planned to load their
gear in the helicopter and head to Bishkek, the capital
of Kyrgyzstan. But before they could do that, they saw
three snowmobiles approaching over the snowy hills.

The Spanns and Lancaster were amazed to see that two of the snowmobile drivers were wearing U.S. Border Patrol outfits. The third was a former Army Ranger now working for the U.S. Department of Homeland Security. The three men were in Kyrgyzstan on a training mission. They had heard that American hunters were stuck in the snow. One of the snowmobilers told the hunters, "We're here to get you guys out."

Tien Shan mountains, Kyrgyzstan

A BAD DECISION

The Spanns and Lancaster decided to take the faster route and fly with the helicopter. They and their Kyrgyz support team piled in, along with what was left of their gear. Spook Spann wondered if the helicopter was overloaded. But before he could say anything, the chopper's motor roared to life. It struggled to get off the ground before finally getting airborne. Once in the air, it zoomed along through the mountain peaks at more than 115 miles (185 km) per hour. But before long, the chopper's rear end began to sag. The pilot asked all the passengers to move forward. But it was too late—the helicopter was too low, and it hit a small hill. It tumbled over and over before crashing to the ground.

The impact left the Spanns briefly unconscious. When they woke, they and Lancaster learned that the pilot and one of their guides had died in the crash. Each of the hunters was injured. Spook and Dennie Spann each struggled to breathe with painful broken ribs. Meanwhile, Lancaster's left eyeball drooped out of its socket. But even with his injured eye, Lancaster was in good shape compared to the others.

With the survivors severely injured, Lancaster was desperate to do something. He took the battery out of his satellite phone and rubbed it hard against his wool pants. He hoped the friction would create enough heat to give the battery a tiny charge—enough to once again call for help. After about 90 minutes of rubbing, he put the battery back in the phone and called the U.S. Embassy in Kyrgyzstan. This time, he was only able to say that the helicopter had crashed and gave a partial location before the line went dead.

That night, the temperatures once again fell to bone-chilling subzero levels. The three hunters slept in the chopper's wreckage. They had given their sleeping bags and extra clothing to the Kyrgyzs. In the morning, Lancaster used duct tape to hold his eye in its socket. He then took a gun and left with one of the guides to find help.

Russian Mi-8 helicopters are usually sturdy and reliable. But the hunters and their gear were too heavy for the chopper to transport safely.

FOUND AT LAST

The pair trudged through snow drifts 3 feet (0.9 m) high.
As they walked, another blizzard set in, and the swirling snow
left Lancaster confused. He thought he was going north, but
when he checked his compass, he realized he was going in the
opposite direction. Trying to find his way through the storm was
even harder with just one eye.

As Lancaster came up a hill, he saw a military base in the
distance. Soon he heard the whine of snowmobiles. When one
of the snowmobiles stopped, Lancaster fired his gun into the sky
twice. The snowmobiler looked in the direction of the shots and
spotted Lancaster. Soon, he and the guide were greeted by three
snowmobilers. They were the same men who had found the
hunters before the helicopter crashed! Lancaster told the men
about the crash, "It's bad—real bad."

The three American snowmobilers transported the injured to
their base at a border crossing station. From there, the hunters
and their guides took trucks to the town of Naryn. But even
then, their ordeal wasn't over. Avalanches in the mountains had
closed the roads, and the Spanns and Lancaster spent several
days in the small town. Finally, they reached Bishkek, the capital
city of Kyrgyzstan. They then flew to Hong Kong for medical
treatment. All three men fully recovered from their injuries after
surviving fierce winter weather that almost left them dead.

At 29,029 feet (8,848 m) high, Mount Everest is the tallest mountain in the world.

DID YOU KNOW?

Skiers, climbers, and others in snowy mountains risk being buried alive by avalanches. These massive flows of snow, ice, and rock can come loose after a heavy snowfall. Once an avalanche begins, it can reach speeds of 80 miles (129 km) per hour in just seconds. Other avalanches are triggered by earthquakes, such as the 7.8 magnitude quake that hit Nepal in 2015. A major avalanche hit the Base Camp at Mount Everest. It killed 21 people. But American journalist Svati Narula survived. She said wind from the avalanche caused most of the damage. "It landed on the back of a uniquely-shaped ridge with such force that some of it ricocheted up and across Base Camp like a bomb blast."

GLOSSARY

buoyancy—the ability of an object to float because it is less dense than the fluid that surrounds it

debris—the remains of something broken or destroyed

epilepsy—an illness that causes people to have blackouts or convulsions

evacuate—to quickly leave a dangerous area and find safety elsewhere

hypothermia—a life-threatening condition that occurs when a person's body temperature falls several degrees below normal

knot—a unit of speed used at sea equal to 1.15 miles (1.85 km) per hour

magnitude—a unit for measuring the amount of energy released by an earthquake

mantle—the layer of hot rock and magma between Earth's crust and the core

radiation—rays of energy given off by certain elements; high doses of radiation can be deadly

refugees—people who are forced to flee their homes because of a natural disaster or war

sewage—water, human waste, and other substances that flow through sewers

supercells—very large and powerful thunderstorms that can produce high winds, large hail, and tornadoes

yacht—a large boat or small ship used for sailing or racing

READ MORE

Monroe Peterson, Judy. *Tornadoes*. New York: Britannica Educational Publishing, 2019.

Shea, Therese. *Rocked by Earthquakes*. New York: PowerKids Press, 2018.

Spilsbury, Louis, and Richard Spilsbury. *Hurricane Hits the Coast*. New York: Gareth Stevens Publishing, 2018.

Waeschle, Amy. *Daring Avalanche Rescues*. North Mankato, MN: Capstone Press, 2018.

INTERNET SITES

Centers for Disease Control and Prevention: Natural Disasters and Severe Weather
https://www.cdc.gov/disasters/index.html

Emergency and Disaster Preparedness
https://www.usa.gov/prepare-for-disasters

National Geographic: Natural Disasters
https://www.nationalgeographic.com/environment/natural-disasters-weather/

National Weather Service: Tornado Survivor Stories
https://www.weather.gov/safety/tornado-survivors

SOURCE NOTES

p. 8, "Get under the tables." "UNMC Fred Ullrich on the Tornado at Boy Scout Camp," YouTube video, University of Nebraska Medical Center, http://www.youtube.com/watch?v=zbsLvmzm_vI, accessed on March 12, 2019.

p. 8, "I hope that's all that happens." "Scout Camp Attendees Recall Storm," WOWT.com, June 13, 2008, https://www.wowt.com/home/headlines/19910214.html, accessed March 12, 2019.

p. 10, "Help is on the way." Sophia Tareen, "Scout Leaders Recount Tornado Experience," *Lincoln Journal Star*, June 12, 2008, https://journalstar.com/news/state-and-regional/govt-and-politics/scout-leaders-recount-tornado-experience/article_1501ab30-fbc4-51e4-9eff-bbd9f03ae34d.html, accessed March 4, 2019.

p. 12, "I had to learn to walk again." Mike Kilen, "A Tornado Took 4 Teenagers' Lives at an Iowa Boy Scouts Camp. Here's How It Reshaped Survivors," *Des Moines Register*, June 9, 2018, https://www.desmoinesregister.com/story/news/2018/06/09/tornado-killed-boy-scouts-changed-lives-iowa/660843002/, accessed on April 14, 2019.

p. 18, "It is time to act . . .," Luis Ferré-Sadurní and Frances Robles, "Puerto Rico Braces for 'Potentially Catastrophic' Hit by Hurricane Maria," *New York Times*, September 19, 2017, https://www.nytimes.com/2017/09/19/us/puerto-rico-hurricane-maria.html, accessed March 29, 2019.

p. 19, "This is a place that floods." Mattathias Schwartz, "Maria's Bodies," *New York*, December 25, 2017, http://nymag.com/intelligencer/2017/12/hurricane-maria-man-made-disaster.html, accessed March 4, 2019.

p. 19, "The river is coming! . . .," Ibid.

p. 20, "Nobody is going to come for us." Ibid.

p. 21, "We were prepared to die." Ibid.

p. 23, "an American hero." Tricia L. Nadolny, "She Saved Her Puerto Rican Neighborhood; Her 'Angels' Flew Her to Philly," *Philadelphia Inquirer*, August 8, 2018, https://www.philly.com/philly/news/politics/puerto-rico-hurricane-maria-philadelphia-milly-chevere-ortiz-20180808.html, accessed March 4, 2019.

p. 25, "I have two children! . . .," "27 Days in Haiti Rubble," *Outlook*, June 1, 2010, BBC Sounds, https://www.bbc.co.uk/sounds/play/p007tf87, accessed April 20, 2019.

p. 28, "There is the slightest sign . . . hope is fading." David Batty, "Haiti Ends Quake Rescue Operations," *The Guardian*, January 23, 2010, https://www.theguardian.com/world/2010/jan/23/haiti-ends-quake-rescue-operations, accessed April 20, 2019.

p. 29, "I could hear people passing by . . .," "Miracle Haiti Earthquake Survivor in Good Health." *CBS News*, January 10, 2011. Available online at https://www.cbsnews.com/news/miracle-haiti-earthquake-survivor-in-good-health/ Accessed on March 29, 2019.

p. 32, "I wonder what it means . . .," Nick Ward and Sinéad O'Brien, *Left for Dead: Surviving the Deadliest Storm in Modern Sailing History*. New York: Bloomsbury USA, 2007, p. 41.

p. 34, "It's building faster than we expected." Ibid., p. 45.

p. 36, "Come on Nick . . .," Ibid., p. 68.

p. 36, "Dad is injured." Ibid., p. 71.

p. 37, "If you ever see . . .," Ibid., p. 87.

p. 41, "Been in my head . . .," Neil Tweedie, "Horror on the High Seas," *Telegraph*, May 26, 2007, https://www.telegraph.co.uk/news/features/3632708/Horror-on-the-high-seas.html, accessed April 13, 2019.

p. 42, "This is a big one . . .," "Japan's Catastrophe and the Disaster That Awaits," *CBS News*, March 22, 2011, https://www.cbsnews.com/news/japans-catastrophe-and-the-disaster-that-awaits/, accessed March 5, 2019.

p. 43, "Tsunami is coming!" Lucy Birmingham and David McNeill, *Strong in the Rain: Surviving Japan's Earthquake, Tsunami, and Fukushima Disaster*. New York: Palgrave Macmillan, 2012, p. 18.

p. 47, "Help us! Help us! Ibid., p. 20.

p. 49, "Hang in there, hang in there." "Japan's Catastrophe and the Disaster That Awaits." *CBS News*, March 22, 2011, https://www.cbsnews.com/news/japans-catastrophe-and-the-disaster-that-awaits/. Accessed March 5, 2019.

p. 53, "It just snowed and snowed. . .," "Blizzard of Death," *I Shouldn't Be Alive*, Daily Motion.com, April 23, 2010, https://www.dailymotion.com/video/x6126w9, accessed May 24, 2019.

p. 54, "It was definitely a concern of mine...," Ibid.

p. 55, "We're here to get you guys out." Ibid.

p. 58, "It's bad—real bad." Jeffrey M. Barker, "Riding to Rescue, Twice, in Kyrgyzstan," *Seattle Post-Intelligencer*, May 16, 2004, https://www.seattlepi.com/local/article/Riding-to-rescue-twice-in-Kyrgyzstan-1144930.php, accessed April 25, 2019.

p. 59, "It landed on the back . . .," Svati Narula, "I Survived the Deadliest Day in Everest's History, and I'm Still Surviving It." *Quartz*, September 25, 2015, http://qz.com/509641/everest-base-camp-avalanche-i-survived-the-deadliest-day-and-im-still-surviving-it/, accessed April 12, 2019.

SELECT BIBLIOGRAPHY

ooks

irmingham, Lucy, and David McNeill. *Strong in ıe Rain: Surviving Japan's Earthquake, Tsunami, ınd Fukushima Disaster.* New York: Palgrave Macmillan, 2012.

Ward, Nick, and Sinéad O'Brien. *Left for Dead: Surviving the Deadliest Storm in Modern Sailing History.* New York: Bloomsbury USA, 2007.

Websites and Articles

Barker, Jeffrey M. "Riding to Rescue, Twice, in Kyrgyzstan," *Seattle Post-Intelligencer*, May 16, 2004, https://www.seattlepi.com/local/article/Riding-to-rescue-twice-in-Kyrgyzstan-1144930.php. Accessed April 25, 2019.

Beser, Ari. "Exclusive: One Man's Harrowing Story of Surviving the Japan Tsunami," National Geographic.org, March 23, 2016, https://blog.nationalgeographic.org/2016/03/23/exclusive-one-mans-harrowing-story-of-surviving-the-japan-tsunami/. Accessed April 22, 2019.

"Blizzard of Death." *I Shouldn't Be Alive*, April 23, 2010, https://www.dailymotion.com/video/x6126w9. Accessed May 24, 2019.

Carroll, Rory. "Haiti Man Rescued After 27 Days in Quake Rubble," *The Guardian*, February 9, 2010, https://www.theguardian.com/world/2010/feb/09/haiti-man-rescued-27-days-rubble. Accessed March 28, 2019.

Cave, Damien, and Deborah Sontagjan. "Rescues Beat Dimming Odds in Haiti but Fall Short of Need," *New York Times*, January 18, 2010, https://www.nytimes.com/2010/01/18/world/americas/18quake.html. Accessed March 28, 2019.

Celoge, Jude. "Haiti: Red Cross Helps to Rescue Darlene," International Committee of the Red Cross, January 28, 2010, https://www.icrc.org/en/doc/resources/documents/feature/2010/haiti-earthquake-feature-280110.htm. Accessed March 28, 2019.

Duffy, Erin. "10 Years Ago, a Tornado Killed 4 Boy Scouts at Little Sioux Camp," *Omaha World-Herald*, June 12, 2018, https://www.omaha.com/news/iowa/years-ago-a-tornado-killed-boy-scouts-at-little-sioux/article_67237b63-6904-5ed3-a261-b069a4215a57.html. Accessed March 26, 2019.

"Eyewitness Accounts from Little Sioux Boy Scout Ranch." *North Platte Telegraph*, June 12, 2008, https://www.nptelegraph.com/breaking_news/eyewitness-accounts-from-little-sioux-boy-scout-ranch/article_8bc8d5f4-0afa-5bd9-ba63-820ea92795c5.html. Accessed March 26, 2019.

"Fastnet 1979." People Features, Cornwall. BBC, May 8, 2009, http://www.bbc.co.uk/cornwall/content/articles/2009/08/05/people_fastnet1979_feature.shtml. Accessed April 14, 2019.

Ferré-Sadurní, Luis, and Frances Robles. "Puerto Rico Braces for 'Potentially Catastrophic' Hit by Hurricane Maria," *New York Times*, September 19, 2017, https://www.nytimes.com/2017/09/19/us/puerto-rico-hurricane-maria.html. Accessed March 29, 2019.

Goddard, Jacqui. "Buried for 27 Days: Haiti Earthquake Survivor's Amazing Story," *Telegraph*, March 28, 2010, https://www.telegraph.co.uk/news/worldnews/centralamericaandthecaribbean/haiti/7530686/Buried-for-27-days-Haiti-earthquake-survivors-amazing-story.html. Accessed April 17, 2019.

Hurricane Maria. FEMA, https://www.fema.gov/hurricane-maria. Accessed March 29, 2019.

"Japan's Catastrophe and the Disaster That Awaits." *CBS News*, March 22, 2011, https://www.cbsnews.com/news/japans-catastrophe-and-the-disaster-that-awaits/2/. Accessed March 5, 2019.

Kilen, Mike. "A Tornado Took 4 Teenagers' Lives at an Iowa Boy Scouts Camp. Here's How It Reshaped Survivors," *Des Moines Register*, June 9, 2018, https://www.desmoinesregister.com/story/news/2018/06/09/tornado-killed-boy-scouts-changed-lives-iowa/660843002/. Accessed April 14, 2019.

"Miracle Haiti Earthquake Survivor in Good Health." *CBS News*, January 10, 2011, https://www.cbsnews.com/news/miracle-haiti-earthquake-survivor-in-good-health/. Accessed March 19, 2019.

Nadolny, Tricia L. "She Saved Her Puerto Rican Neighborhood; Her 'Angels' Flew Her to Philly," *Philadelphia Inquirer*, August 8, 2018, https://www.philly.com/philly/news/politics/puerto-rico-hurricane-maria-philadelphia-milly-chevere-ortiz-20180808.html. Accessed March 4, 2019.

Paterson, Tony. "Hell and High Water: The Fastnet Disaster." *The Independent*, July 18, 2009, https://www.independent.co.uk/sport/general/sailing/hell-and-high-water-the-fastnet-disaster-1748093.html. Accessed April 19, 2019.

Schwartz Mattathias, "Maria's Bodies." *New York*, December 25, 2017, http://nymag.com/intelligencer/2017/12/hurricane-maria-man-made-disaster.html. Accessed March 4, 2019.

"Scout Camp Attendees Recall Storm." WOWT.com, Jun 13, 2008, https://www.wowt.com/home/headlines/19910214.html. Accessed March 12, 2019.

Tweedie, Neil. "Horror on the High Seas," *Telegraph*, May 26, 2007, https://www.telegraph.co.uk/news/features/3632708/Horror-on-the-high-seas.html. Accessed April 13, 2019.

Webster, Donovan. "Death in the Tien Shan." *Field and Stream*, October 2004.

INDEX

ABOUT THE AUTHOR

Michael Burgan has written numerous books for children and young adults during his nearly 20 years as a freelance author. Many of his books have focused on U.S. history, geography, and world leaders. He has also written fiction and adapted classic novels for children. Michael graduated from the University of Connecticut with a degree in history. He lives in Santa Fe, New Mexico.